Envisioning Art:
A Collection of
Quotations by Artists

Envisioning Art:
A Collection of
Quotations by Artists

Edited by William C. MacKay

BARNES
&NOBLE
BOOKS
NEW YORK

To Hugh Kenner, long distance mentor
and in memory of dear friend Edwin Denby
(1903-1983)

The author wishes to thank artists, writers, and dancers
too numerous to name for their aesthetic explorations. I want
to thank also my colleagues and contributors Rick Campbell;
Heather Russell-Revesz; Sharon Bosley; Mike Ferrari; and,
most especially, Ellen MacKay Pease and Maureen Slattery.

The quotes in this book have been drawn from many
sources, and are assumed to be accurate as quoted in their
previously published forms. Although every effort has been
made to verify the quotes and sources, the publisher
cannot guarantee their perfect accuracy.

2003 Barnes & Noble Books

ISBN 0-7607-4055-0

Printed and bound in the United States of America

M 9 8 7 6 5 4 3 2 1

Method of this project: literary montage. I needn't say anything. Merely show. I shall purloin no valuables, appropriate no ingenious formulations. But the rags, the refuse—these I will not inventory but allow, in the only way possible, to come into their own: by making use of them.

—WALTER BENJAMIN

CONTEMPORARY ARTISTS LIVE IN A WORLD OF ECHOES. Snippets of past masters surface on their canvases or in their poems and beloved texts billow up on their computers. Composers weave disparate melodies into symphony pieces; post-modern choreographers "quote" movements of Balanchine and Petipa in downtown concerts. Indeed, the past century has been an age of quotation and counterfeit, ushered in by the trembling resonance of T.S. Eliot's *The Wasteland* and James Joyce's sly *Odyssey* set in downtown Dublin.

"*These fragments I have shored against my ruins,*" Eliot wrote, echoing Elizabethan playwright Thomas Kyd, but for many of us, these fragments breathe new life into our being. The description of a Robert Rauschenberg collage reads like an inventory of flotsam; but combined, the *"oil, watercolor, pencil, crayon, paper, fabric, photographs, printed reproductions, miniature blueprint, metal, newspaper, glass, dried grass and steel wool, with pillow, wood post, electric lights, and Plymouth Rock rooster, on wood structure mounted on four casters"* effect an odd alchemy.

In the spirit of that joyful disorder, I assembled this word salad without regard to genre, medium, or preset rhythm. Agreeing with the spirit of Picasso's comment that "sculpture is the best comment that a painter can make on painting", I mingled quotations about architecture and poetry with those about music and dance. As Marc Chagall said, "work in whatever medium likes me at the moment." Creativity is promiscuous.

The sequence of the quotations is intentional, but not irrevocable. In gathering the book, I followed the procedure of Hugh Kenner (who, in turn, picked it up from Marshall McLuhan): I gisted quotations onto little slips; let their affinities prompt the piles they went into; and then constructed little strings of incitement. I invite readers to construct their own quotation books or family dramas from these tidbits.

–W.C.M.

White. A blank page or canvas. So many possibilities.

—STEPHEN SONDHEIM AND JAMES LAPINE

All art is the same—an attempt to fill an empty space.

—SAMUEL BECKETT

The last thing one discovers in composing a work is what to put first.

—BLAISE PASCAL

I have invented myself entirely: a childhood, a personality, longings, dreams and memories, all in order to enable me to tell them.

—FEDERICO FELLINI

Color possesses me. I don't have to pursue it. It will possess me always. I know it. This is the meaning of the happy hour. Color and I are one. I am a painter.

—PAUL KLEE

Painting is dancing with chaos.

—MELANIE CIRCLE

There is a bit of insanity in dancing that does everybody a good deal of good.

—Edwin Denby

To be an artist means to never avert one's eyes.

—Marcus Claudius Marcellus

We work in the dark—we do what we can—we give what we have. Our doubt is our passion, and our passion is our task. The rest is the madness of art.

—Henry James

I throw down the gauntlet to chance. For example, I prepare the ground for a picture by cleaning my brush over the canvas. Spilling a little turpentine can also be helpful.

—JOAN MIRÓ

Make a drawing; begin it again; trace it; begin it again and trace it again.

—EDGAR DÉGAS

If a man throws himself out of the fourth floor window, and you can't make a sketch of him before he gets to the ground, you will never do anything big.

—EUGÉNE DELACROIX

I am simply conscious of the forces I am using and I am driven on by an idea that I really only gasp as it grows with the picture.

—HENRI MATISSE

Dance first. Think later. It's the natural order.

—SAMUEL BECKETT

Don't play what's there, play what's not there.

—MILES DAVIS

You cannot hear the waterfall if you stand next to it. I paint my jungles in the desert.

—MACEDONLO DE LA TORRE

Art is the sex of the imagination.

—George Jean Nathan

Intercourse is what goes on in the sentence. In every sentence the little word "is" is the copula, the penis or bridge; in every sentence magically, with a word, making the two one flesh.

—Norman O. Brown

All art is erotic... A horizontal stroke: the woman lying down. A vertical stroke: the male who penetrates her.

—Adolf Loos

Art should be cold.

—ARNOLD SCHOENBERG

The progress of an artist is a continual self-sacrifice, a continual extinction of personality.

—T. S. ELIOT

A work can have in it a pent-up energy, an intense life of its own, independent of the subject it may represent.

—HENRY MOORE

If it looks like art, chances are it's somebody else's art.

—CHUCK CLOSE

A painting has a life of its own. I try to let it come through.

—JACKSON POLLOCK

The essence of drawing is the line exploring space.

—ANDY GOLDSWORTHY

In life, as in art, the beautiful moves in curves.

—EDWARD BULWER-LYTTON

A picture is not thought out and settled beforehand. While it is being done it changes as one's thoughts change.

—PABLO PICASSO

A line is a dot out for a stroll.

—PAUL KLEE

They despise my novelty, I their timidity.

—EERO SAARINEN

Writing is nothing but a guided dream.

—JORGE LUIS BORGES

Art is our chief means of breaking bread with the dead.

—W. H. AUDEN

If you get an image, try to destroy it.

—RICHARD DIEBENKORN

Painting is, literally, the primal impulse to mark. It's such a clear way of formulating what's inside one's head; it's the most direct way of communication.

—ANNA BIALOBRODA

If my husband ever met a woman on the street who looked like one of his paintings, he would faint.

—JACQUELINE ROQUE, wife of Pablo Picasso

There is a right physical size for every idea.

—HENRY MOORE

I'd rather learn from one bird how to sing than to teach ten thousand stars how not to dance.

—E. E. CUMMINGS

A bird doesn't sing because it has an answer, it sings because it has a song.

—MAYA ANGELOU

My way is to seize an image the moment it has formed in my mind, to trap it as a bird and to pin it at once to canvas. Afterward I start to tame it, to master it. I bring it under control and I develop it.

—JOAN MIRÓ

I applied streaks and blobs of colors onto the canvas with a palette knife and I made them sing with all the intensity I could.

—Wassily Kandinsky

I would rather see the portrait of a dog that I know, than all the allegorical paintings they can show me in the world.

—Samuel Johnson

A pictorial work…is constructed bit by bit, just like a house.

—Paul Klee

Art is not a mirror held up to reality, but a hammer with which to shape it.

—BERTOLT BRECHT

Romance extends actuality; realism examines it. There is no need to choose.

—DELMORE SCHWARTZ

Art must take reality by surprise.

—FRANCOISE SAGAN

Fantasy, abandoned by reason, produces impossible monsters; united with it, she is the mother of the arts and the origin of marvels.

—GOYA

Meaning is not in things but in between; in the iridescence, in the interplay; in the interconnections at the intersections, at the crossroads.

—Norman O. Brown

In a free society art is not a weapon...Artists are not engineers of the soul.

—John F. Kennedy

No amount of skillful invention can replace the essential element of imagination.

—Edward Hopper

A picture is first of all a product of the imagination of the artist; it must never be a copy.

—EDGAR DÉGAS

I don't paint things; I paint the difference between things.

—HENRI MATISSE

Art takes what in life is an accidental pleasure and tries to repeat and prolong it.

—EDWIN DENBY

All art is a kind of confession, more or less oblique. All artists, if they are to survive, are forced at last to tell the whole story; to vomit the anguish up.

—JAMES BALDWIN

Unfinished paintings are more admired than the finished because the artist's actual thoughts are left visible.

—PLINY

I refrain from 'finishing' [the artwork]. I paint myself out of the picture, and when I have done that, I either throw it away or keep it.

—WILLEM deKOONING

The artist, like the God of creation, remains within or behind or beyond or above his handiwork, invisible, refined out of existence, indifferent, paring his fingernails.

—JAMES JOYCE

Given a source of energy which you can direct, you can direct yourself out of the picture.

—JACK SPICER

An artist cannot speak about his art any more than a plant can discuss horticulture.

—JEAN COCTEAU

I passionately hate the idea of being with it, I think an artist has always to be out of step with his time.

—ORSON WELLES

The composer creates time and we have to dance to it.

—GEORGE BALANCHINE

Let us return to old times and that will be progress!

—IGOR STRAVINSKY

Perhaps my whisper was already born before my lips.

—OSIP MANDELSTAM

Every great work, of art has two faces, one toward its own time and one toward the future, toward eternity.

—DANIEL BARENBOIM

We invent the past and remember the future.

—ISAK DINESEN

Surely all art is the result of one's having been in danger, of having gone through an experience all the way to the end, where no one can go any further.

—RAINER MARIA RILKE

Music, when soft voices die, vibrates in the memory.

—PERCY BYSSHE SHELLEY

Now I'm dead in the grave with my lips moving
And every schoolboy repeating my words by
heart.

—Osip Mandelstam

Fortunately art is a community effort—a small but select community living in a spiritualized world endeavoring to interpret the wars and the solitudes of the flesh.

—Allen Ginsberg

One has a nose. The nose scents and it chooses. An artist is simply a kind of pig snouting truffles.

—Igor Stravinsky

Artists are the antennae of the human race, but the bullet-headed many will never learn to trust their great artists.

—Ezra Pound

Being the antennae of the race sounds like a job for the secret police.

—W. H. Auden

The essential difference between art and spying is that in art, you share all the secrets.

—Caleb Jackson

All art is subversive.

—Pablo Picasso

Art is either plagiarism or revolution.

—PAUL GAUGUIN

Dancing is like bank robbery. It takes split second timing.

—TWYLA THARP

The moment you cheat for the sake of beauty, you know you're an artist.

—MAX JACOB

Immature poets imitate; mature poets steal.

—T. S. ELIOT

Writing is a form of personal freedom. It frees us from the mass identity we see in the making all around us. In the end, writers will write not to be outlaw heroes of some under-culture but mainly to save themselves, to survive as individuals.

—Don DeLillo

Art is the only work open to people who can't get along with others and still want to be special.

—Alasdair Gray

In the cave paintings at Lascaux, the only creature who looks like an intruder is the human.

—Caleb Jackson

'Painting' and 'religious experience' are the same thing. It is a question of the perpetual motion of a right idea.

—BEN NICHOLSON

Art is a collaboration between God and the artist, and the less the artist does the better.

—ANDRE GIDE

The neutrality and clarity of an engineering drawing is a better model for teaching about art than all the uncontrollable drivel about the cabbala and metaphysics and the ecstasy of sainthood.

—GEORGE GROSZ

Art is the human disposition of sensible or intelligible matter for an esthetic end.

—JAMES JOYCE

To find a form that accommodates the mess, that is the task of the artist now.

—SAMUEL BECKETT

Form is an endless effort, and not only that, but perhaps the secret of life.

—DELMORE SCHWARTZ

I prefer the emotion that corrects the rule.

—JUAN GRIS

Art is the imposing of a pattern on experience, and our aesthetic enjoyment is recognition of the pattern.

—ALFRED NORTH WHITEHEAD

Art is so wonderfully irrational, exuberantly pointless, but necessary all the same.

—GÜNTER GRASS

Poetry, you put storms to good use.

—OSIP MANDELSTAM

I must create a system
Or be enslaved by another man's;
I will not reason and compare;
My business is to create.

—WILLIAM BLAKE

Organic buildings are the strength and lightness of the spiders' spinning, buildings qualified by light, bred by native character to environment, married to the ground.

—FRANK LLOYD WRIGHT

Architecture is frozen music.

—JOHANN WOLFGANG VAN GOETHE

Dance is music made visible.

—GEORGE BALANCHINE

Dance is discovery, discovery, discovery.

—MARTHA GRAHAM

Music begins to atrophy when it departs too far from the dance…poetry begins to atrophy when it gets too far from music.

—EZRA POUND

Music is a means of rapid transportation.

—JOHN CAGE

Harmony consists of opposing tension, like that of the bow and the lyre.

—HERACLITUS

Photography is nature seen from the eyes outwards. Painting is nature seen from the eyes inwards.

—CHARLES SHEELER

The painter disputes and competes with nature.

—LEONARDO DA VINCI

Photography freed painting from a lot of tiresome chores, starting with family portraits.

—PIERRE AUGUSTE RENOIR

It's really absurd to make an image, like a human image, with paint, today, when you think about it... But then all of a sudden, it was even more absurd not to do it.

—WILLEM DE KOONING

All good drama has two movements, first the making of the mistake, then the discovery that it was a mistake.

—W. H. AUDEN

Theatre is like operating with a scalpel. Film is operating with a laser.

—MICHAEL CAINE

If I were a writer, how I would enjoy being told the novel is dead. How liberating to work in the margins, outside a central perception. You are the ghoul of literature. Lovely.

—DON DeLILLO

Words are what sticks to the real. We use them to push the real, to drag the real into the poem. They are what we hold on with, nothing else. They are as valuable in themselves as rope with nothing to be tied to.

—JACK SPICER

A portrait is a picture in which there is just a tiny little something not quite right about the mouth.

—JOHN SINGER SARGENT

There are only two styles of portrait painting: the serious and the smirk.

—CHARLES DICKENS

Detail is the heart of realism, and the fatty degeneration of art.

—CLIVE BELL

Life doesn't imitate art. It imitates bad television.

—WOODY ALLEN

There can be no transformation of reality where there is no imitation of reality: minute attention.

—DELMORE SCHWARTZ

Art, indeed, began with abstraction.

—S. Giedion

Interpretation in art is the revenge of the intellect.

—Susan Sontag

The more minimal the art, the more maximum the explanation.

—Hilton Kramer

Painting: The art of protecting flat surfaces from the weather and exposing them to critics.

—Ambrose Bierce

A poem is a ritual referring to divine orders.

—ROBERT DUNCAN

That which is static and repetitive is boring. That which is dynamic and random is confusing. In between lies art.

—JOHN LOCKE

The hidden harmony is better than the obvious.

—ALEXANDER POPE

Impressionism is the newspaper of the soul.

—HENRI MATISSE

It is difficult
to get the news from poems
yet men die miserably every day
for lack
of what is found there.

—WILLIAM CARLOS WILLIAMS

Literature is news that STAYS news.

—EZRA POUND

All art is advertising. It stands for a particular point of view. Art that exploits badness is advertising badness.

—JACK BEAL

A work of art that contains theories is like an object on which the price tag remains.

—MARCEL PROUST

Art never expresses anything but itself.

—OSCAR WILDE

Art cannot be above the battle.

—HOWARD TAUBMAN

My dear Tristan, to be an artist at all is like living in Switzerland during a world war.

—TOM STOPPARD

Art advances between two chasms, which are frivolity and propaganda. On the ridge where the great artist moves forward, every step is an adventure, an extreme risk. In that risk, however, and only there, lies the freedom of art.

—ALBERT CAMUS

The aim of every artist is to arrest motion, which is life, by artificial means and hold it fixed so that a hundred years later, when a stranger looks at it, it moves again, since it is life.

—WILLIAM FAULKNER

Shall I tell you what I think are the two qualities of a work of art? First, it must be the indescribable, and second, it must be inimitable.

—PIERRE AUGUSTE RENOIR

Art is a lie which makes us realize the truth.

—Pablo Picasso

Art is just another way of keeping a diary.

—Pablo Picasso

There is no accident, just as there is no beginning and no end.

—Jackson Pollock

Art teaches nothing but the significance of life.

—Henry Miller

It is through art, and through art only, that we can realize our perfection; through art and art only that we can shield ourselves from the sordid perils of actual existence.

—OSCAR WILDE

There is the view that poetry should improve your life. I think people confuse it with the Salvation Army.

—JOHN ASHBERY

Artists to my mind are the real architects of change, and not the political legislators who implement change after the fact.

—WILLIAM S. BURROUGHS

The artist's business is to feel, although he may think a little sometimes…when he has nothing better to do.

—JOHN RUSKIN

All poets adore explosions, thunderstorms, tornadoes, conflagrations, ruins, scenes of spectacular carnage. The poetic imagination is therefore not at all a desirable quality in a chief of state.

—W. H. AUDEN

I am tortured by the endlessness of the particular.

—DELMORE SCHWARTZ

Be attentive to the minute particular.

—WILLIAM BLAKE

Each thing implies the universe.

—JORGE LUIS BORGES

No ideas but in things.

—WILLIAM CARLOS WILLIAMS

An artist who has no imagination is a mechanic.

—ROBERT HENRI

The ultimate aim of all visual arts is the complete building!

—Walter Gropius

Art completes what nature cannot bring to a finish.

—Aristotle

You come to nature with all her theories, and she knocks them all flat.

—Pierre Auguste Renoir

The job of the artist is always to deepen the mystery.

—Francis Bacon

Trash has given us an appetite for art.

—PAULINE KAEL

Art washes away from the soul the dust of every-day life.

—PABLO PICASSO

All the best works of any artist must be bathed, so to speak, in mystery.

—AUGUSTE RODIN

Every canvas, even if non-representational that depends upon harmonious relationships of the three forces (color, volume and line) is a work of art.

—FERNAND LÉGER

Art is the proper task of life.

—FRIEDRICH NIETZSCHE

There are two kinds of taste, the taste for emotions of surprise and the taste for emotions of recognition.

—HENRY JAMES

Taste is the death of a painter.

—WALTER SICKERT

In my studio I'm as happy as a cow in her stall. That's the only place where everything is all right.

—LOUISE NEVELSON

I think most artists create out of despair. The very nature of creation is not a performing glory on the outside, it's a painful, difficult search within.

—Louise Nevelson

No one has ever written or painted, sculpted, modeled, built, invented, except to get out of hell.

—Antonin Artaud

With an eye made quiet by the power of harmony, and the deep power of joy, we see into the life of things.

—William Wordsworth

I don't want people who want to dance, I want people who have to dance.

—George Balanchine

For me, a landscape does not exist in its own right, since its appearances changes every moment.

—Claude Monet

Drawing is the honesty of the art. There is no possibility of cheating: It is either good or bad.

—Salvador Dali

Art, whose honesty must work through artifice, cannot avoid cheating truth.

—Laura Riding

I saw the angel in the marble and carved until I set him free.

—MICHELANGELO

I choose a block of marble and chop off whatever I don't need.

—AUGUSTE RODIN

I suppose I am basically a clerk, a cataloguer. I like the reductiveness of that, I like the stripping down, the basic form of organization.

—PETER GREENAWAY

The brush is a more powerful and rapid tool than the point or the stump...the main thing that the brush secures is the instant grasp of the grand construction of a figure.

—THOMAS EAKINS

The artist never entirely knows. We guess. We may be wrong, but we take leap after leap in the dark.

—AGNES DE MILLE

I do not pose my sitters. I do not deliberate and then concoct. Before painting, when I talk to the person, they unconsciously assume their most characteristic pose, which in a way involves all their character and social standing—what the world has done to them and their retaliation.

—ALICE NEEL

Lay down these words
Before your mind like rocks.
placed solid, by hands
In choice of place, set
Before the body of the mind
in space and time.

—GARY SNYDER

When you can experience eternity instead of
time...when you get the eternity of waking up in
the night, and then look at the clock and five
minutes have passed instead on an hour, it's a
mockery of eternity.

—JOSEPH CORNELL

Do not quench your inspiration and your imagination; do not become the slave of your model.

—VINCENT VAN GOGH

My models, my human figures, are never like extras in an interior. They are the main theme of my work. I depend absolutely on my model.

—Henri Matisse

Model: Between you and him, not just to reduce but to suppress the distance.

—Robert Bresson

I hate flowers. I only paint them because they're cheaper than models and they don't move.

—Georgia O'Keefe

The more I become decomposed, the more sick and fragile I am, the more I become an artist.

—Vincent Van Gogh

Saying that a great genius is mad, while at the same time recognizing his artistic worth, is like saying that he had rheumatism or suffered from diabetes.

—James Joyce

His art is the health of the artist.

—Harold Clurman

An artist has been defined as a neurotic who continually cures himself with his art.

—LEE SIMONSON

Surely all art is the result of one's having been in danger, of having gone through an experience all the way to the end, where no one can go any further.

—RAINER MARIA RILKE

It takes a lot of time to be a genius, you have to sit around so much doing nothing really doing nothing.

—GERTRUDE STEIN

Thanks to art, instead of seeing a single realm, our own, we see it multiply until we have before us as many worlds as there are original artists.

—MARCEL PROUST

Do not imagine that art is something which is designed to give gentle uplift and self-confidence. Art is not a brassiere. At least, not in the English sense. But do not forget that brassiere is the French word for life-jacket.

—JULIAN BARNES

Each energy calls for its complementary energy to achieve self-contained stability based on the play of energies.

—PAUL KLEE

Irresponsibility is part of the pleasure of all arts.

—PAULINE KAEL

The true artist will let his wife starve, his children go barefoot, his mother drudge for his living at seventy, sooner than work at anything but his art.

—GEORGE BERNARD SHAW

In order to create there must be a dynamic force, and what force is more potent than love?

—IGOR STRAVINSKY

I shall state silences more competently than ever a better man spangled the butterflies of vertigo.

—SAMUEL BECKETT

I decided it is better to scream… Silence is the real crime against humanity.

—Nadezhda Mandelstam

One never paints violently enough.

—Eugéne Delacroix

There are no solutions. History solved nothing. Nothing…. For I do not give solutions, either, no answers, I only ask questions, in a tattling way. I talk much, much, very much, in order to disrupt language. I pitch into ideas by the uproar of the word.

—Eugéne Ionesco

I have nothing to say and I am saying it.

—JOHN CAGE

I have simply wished to assert the reasoned and independent feeling of my individuality within a total knowledge of tradition.

—HENRI MATISSE

I want to leave everything as it is. I therefore neither plan nor invent: I add nothing and omit nothing. I steer clear of definitions. I do not know what I want.

—GERHARD RICHTER

Western art is built on the biographical passion of one artist for another.

—JIM DINE

Every master knows that the material teaches the artist.

—ILYA EHRENBERG

You begin with the possibilities of the material, and then you see what they can do, so the artist is almost a bystander while he's working.

—ROBERT RAUSCHENBERG

The big artist keeps a sharp eye on nature and steals her tools... Then he's got a canoe of his own, smaller than nature's but big enough for every purpose.... With this canoe he can sail parallel to nature's sailing.

—THOMAS EAKINS

Any tool you use is legitimate. The key to the tool is whether it has the dimensions to deal with what have become your questions.

—ROBERT IRWIN

The biographer may be as imaginative as he pleases—the more imaginative the better—in the way in which he brings together his materials, but he must not imagine the materials.

—LEON EDEL

Reality is that which, when you stop believing in it, doesn't go away.

—Philip K. Dick

When one starts from a portrait and seeks by successive eliminations to find pure form...one inevitably ends up with an egg.

—Pablo Picasso

When painting the faces of young persons...use the yolk of the egg of a city hen, because they have lighter yolks than those of country hens.

—Cennino Cennini

A portrait is a picture in which there is just a tiny little something not quite right about the mouth.

—JOHN SINGER SARGENT

There is no abstract art. You must always start with something. Afterward you can remove all traces of reality.

—PABLO PICASSO

A curve does not exist in its full power until contrasted with a straight line.

—ROBERT HENRI

Always lines, never forms. But where do they find these lines in nature? For my part, I see only forms that are lit up and forms that are not. There is only line and shadow.

—GOYA

The object of art is to give life a shape.

—JEAN ANOUILH

A shadow is always effected by the color of the surface on which it is cast.

—LEONARDO DA VINCI

Colors speak all languages.

—JOSEPH ADDISON

Look for echoes. Sometimes the same shape or direction will echo through the picture.

—ROBERT HENRI

Form is the shape of content.

—BEN SHAHN

Color is all. When color is right, form is right. Color is everything, color is vibration like music; everything is vibration.

—MARC CHAGALL

Draw with the brush. Carve the form. Don't be carried away by subtleties of modeling and nice pigmentation at the expense of losing the form.

—JOHN SLOAN

I organize the opposition between colors, lines and curves. I set curves against straight lines, patches of color against plastic forms, pure colors against subtly nuanced shades of gray.

—FERNAND LÉGER

Lines are results; do not draw them for themselves.

—ROBERT HENRI

Writing means revealing oneself to excess.

—Franz Kafka

The principles of parsimony is valid esthetically in that the artist must not go beyond what is needed for his purpose.

—Rudolf Arnheim

In a big picture you see what o'clock it is, afternoon or morning, if it is hot or cold, winter or summer, and what kind of people are there, and what they are doing and why they are doing it.

—Thomas Eakins

What modern man wants is the grin without the cat, the sensation without the boredom of its conveyance.

—PAUL VALERY

What shall I love if not the enigma?

—GIORGIO DE CHIRICO

The nature of the work is to prepare for a good accident.

—SIDNEY LUMET

Dialogue should simply be a sound among other sounds, just something that comes out of the mouths of people whose eyes tell the story in visual terms.

—ALFRED HITCHCOCK

Life is not what is said, but the process of saying, not the created picture, but the creating.

—GERHARD RICHTER

When you see a fish you don't think of its scales, do you? You think of its speed; its floating, flashing body seen through the water... If I made fins and eyes and scales, I would arrest its movement, give a pattern or shape of reality. I want just the flash of its spirit.

—CONSTANTIN BRANCUSI

Dreams form the bristles of the artist's brush. In trying to probe beyond the ordinary and the common... I probe beyond the confines of the finite to create an infinite. Liver. Bone. Living rocks and living plants and animals.

—ARSHILE GORKY

Art has the suddenness, the audacity, and sometimes the savagery of impolite wit.

—CALEB JACKSON

Laughter is a reaction against rigidity.

—HANS RICHTER

Surprise laughs wildly in the purity of light.

—GIULLAUME APOLLINAIRE, ON HENRI MATISSE

The first prerogative of an artist in any medium is to make a fool of himself.

—PAULINE KAEL

My brush stroke has no system at all. I hit the canvas with irregular touches of the brush, which I leave as they are. Patches of thickly laid-on color, spots of canvas left bare, here and there portions are left absolutely unfinished, repetitions, savageries; in short, I am inclined to think that result is so disquieting and irritating as to be a godsend to those people who have fixed conceptions about technique.

—VINCENT VAN GOGH

Every page must explode, whether through seriousness, profundity, turbulence, nausea, the news, the eternal, annihilating nonsense, enthusiasm for principles, or the way it is printed. Art must be unaesthetic in the extreme; useless; impossible to justify.

—Francis Picabia

It's when you've found out how to do certain things, that it's time to stop doing them, because what's missing is that you're not including the risk.

—Robert Rauschenberg

I want to be as though newborn, knowing nothing, absolutely nothing... Then I want to do something modest; to work out by myself a tiny, formal motive, one that my pencil will be able to hold without technique.

—Paul Klee

If you think of a school drawing while you work, your drawing will look like one.

—Robert Henri

Art class was like a religious ceremony to me. I would wash my hands carefully before touching paper or pencils. The instruments of work were sacred objects to me.

—Joan Miró

An art school is a place for young girls to pass the time between high school and marriage.

—Thomas Hart Benton

At the age of six I wanted to be a cook. At seven I wanted to be Napoleon. And my ambition has been growing steadily ever since.

—LOUISE BOURGEOIS

Color is like cooking. The cook puts in more or less salt, that's the difference

—JOSEF ALBERS

Many excellent cooks are spoiled by going into the arts.

—PAUL GAUGUIN

For me, cinema is not a slice of life, but a piece of cake.

—ALFRED HITCHCOCK

Never talk about our secret methods. If we talk about them, they stop working.

—JEAN COCTEAU

After silence that which comes nearest to expressing the inexpressible is music.

—ALDOUS HUXLEY

Whoever wishes to devote himself to painting should begin by cutting out his tongue.

—HENRI MATISSE

To achieve harmony in bad taste is the height of elegance.

—JEAN GENET

The position of the artist is humble. He is essentially a channel.

—PIET MONDRIAN

The big artist keeps an eye on nature and steals her tools.

—THOMAS EAKINS

To all appearances, the artist acts like a mediumistic being who, from the labyrinth beyond time and space, seeks his way out to a clearing.

—MARCEL DUCHAMP

Artists are God's little pickpockets.

—CALEB JACKSON

If I didn't start painting, I would have raised chickens.

—GRANDMA MOSES

The real composer thinks about his work the whole time. He is not always conscious of this, but he is aware of it later when he suddenly knows what he will do.

—IGOR STRAVINSKY

Every child is an artist. The problem is how to remain an artist once they grow up.

—PABLO PICASSO

Shadow boxes become poetic theaters or settings wherein are metamorphosed the element of a childhood pastime.

—JOSEPH CORNELL

Poetry is the ultimate small business, requiring a careful keeping of accounts to stay afloat.

—CHARLES BERNSTEIN

Painting is manual labor, no different from any other; it can be done well or poorly.

—GEORGE GROSZ

Art and business may be strange bedfellows, but an artist must make room in bed for both.

—ERIC MAISEL

Money and art
are far apart.

—LANGSTON HUGHES

Art is making something out of nothing and selling it.

—FRANK ZAPPA

Art is man's expression of his joy in labor.

—WILLIAM MORRIS

To be great, art has to point somewhere.

—ANNE LAMOTT

It is art, and art only, that reveals us to ourselves.

—OSCAR WILDE

The space within becomes the reality of the building.

—FRANK LLOYD WRIGHT

More is less.

—MIES VAN DER ROHE

Less is more.

—LE CORBUSIER

If you can talk about it, why paint it?

—FRANCIS BACON

Art is the expression of the profoundest thoughts in the simplest way.

—ALBERT EINSTEIN

Art is science made clear.

—JEAN COCTEAU

In theory there is no difference between theory and practice. In practice there is.

—YOGI BERRA

You know it's very hard to maintain a theory in the face of life that comes crashing about you.

—ALICE NEEL

I have always tried to hide my efforts and wished my works to have the light joyousness of spring-time which never lets anyone suspect the labors it has cost me.

—Henri Matisse

When I see a Frans Hals I feel like painting; but when I see a Rembrandt I feel like giving up.

—Max Liebermann

I remember one day when Juan Gris told me about a bunch of grapes he had seen in a painting by Picasso. The next days these grapes appeared in a painting by Gris, this time in a bowl; and the day after that, the bowl appeared in a painting by Picasso.

—Jacques Lipchitz

Great art is always an invention that begins as an imitation.

—OCTAVIO PAZ

You pour the paint on the snow and take photographs while it melts. All the time it melts, it changes.

—SARI DIENES

Paul Klee is fortunate in never having done a major work; each individual thought as it comes to us trembling with wit and sensibility seems to be all of him.

—FRANK O'HARA

There is nothing so loathsome as a sentimental surrealist.

—THOMAS PYNCHON

Bonnard at times seems styleless. Someone said of him that he had the rare ability to forget from one day to another what he had done. He added the next day's experience to it, like a child following a balloon.

—FRANZ KLINE

For Arp, art is Arp.

—MARCEL DUCHAMP, on Hans Arp

Art is coming face to face with yourself. That's what's wrong with [Thomas Hart] Benton. He came face to face with Michelangelo—and he lost.

—JACKSON POLLOCK

He bores me. He should have stuck to his flying machine.

—PIERRE AUGUSTE RENOIR, on Leonardo Da Vinci

Judges, policemen, critics: These are the real Lower Orders, the low, sly lives, whom no decent person should receive in his house.

—W. H. AUDEN

[Abstract art is] a product of the untalented, sold by the unprincipled to the utterly bewildered.

—AL CAPP

One of the most striking signs of the decay of art is evident when we sees its separate forms jumbled together.

—JOHANN WOLFGANG VAN GOETHE

Scissors, paste, images and genius in effect superseded brushes paint, models, style, sensibility and that famous sincerity demanded of artists.

—RÉNE MAGRITTE

Freedom is poetry, taking liberties with words, breaking the rules of normal speech, violating common sense. Freedom is violence.

—Norman O. Brown

The day is coming when a single carrot, freshly observed, will set off a revolution.

—Paul Cézanne

No one is an artist unless he carries his picture in his head before painting it, and is sure of his method and composition.

—Claude Monet

Only when he no longer knows what he is doing does the painter do good things.

—Edgar Degas

Simplicity is not an end, but one arrives at simplicity in spite of oneself, in approaching the real sense of things.

—Constantin Brancusi

Simplicity and repose are the qualities that measure the true value of any work of art.

—Frank Lloyd Wright

All my work keeps going like a pendulum. It seems to swing back to something I was involved with earlier, or it moves between horizontality and verticality; circularity, or a compose of them. For me, change is the only constant.

—LEE KRASNER

Creativity advances through works that bring about the artist's continuing self-creation.

—GARRY WILLS

All in all, the creative act is not performed by the artist alone; the spectator brings the work in contact with the external world by deciphering and interpreting its inner qualification and thus adds his contribution to the creative act.

—MARCEL DUCHAMP

The spectator can, if he likes it, go out and do his own picking. This teeming obsession that I cannot help having, of benefiting aged people and handicapped children—boxes I have kept purposely in 'etat brut'—a kind of metaphysique of exploration that anyone can do—this kind of thing has a potential for the young blood instead of the museum kind of thing.

—JOSEPH CORNELL

To have great poets, there must be great audiences.

—WALT WHITMAN

I shut my eyes in order to see.

—PAUL GAUGUIN

Cover the canvas at the first go, then work at it until you see nothing more to add.

—CAMILLE PISSARRO

At some point in life the world's beauty becomes enough. You don't need to photograph, paint it, or even remember it. It is enough.

—TONI MORRISON

The antimony between mind and body, word and deed, speech and silence, overcome. Everything is only a metaphor; there is only poetry.

—NORMAN O. BROWN

Do not finish your work too much. An impression is not sufficiently durable for its first freshness to survive a belated search for infinite detail.

—PAUL GAUGUIN

To achieve vital harmony in a picture it must be constructed out of parts in themselves incomplete, brought into harmony only at the last stroke.

—PAUL KLEE